SandCastle™

Team Sports
By the Numbers

Volleyball
By the Numbers

Colleen Dolphin

Consulting Editor, Diane Craig, M.A./Reading Specialist

ABDO
Publishing Company

Published by ABDO Publishing Company, 8000 West 78th Street, Edina, Minnesota 55439.

Copyright © 2010 by Abdo Consulting Group, Inc. International copyrights reserved in all countries.

No part of this book may be reproduced in any form without written permission from the publisher. SandCastle™ is a trademark and logo of ABDO Publishing Company.

Printed in the United States.

 PRINTED ON RECYCLED PAPER

Editor: Liz Salzmann
Content Developer: Nancy Tuminelly
Cover and Interior Design and Production: Colleen Dolphin, Mighty Media
Photo Credits: iStockphoto (Judi Ashlock, Charles Benavidez, Jon Brewer, Stephan Hoerold), Shutterstock, Rubberball Productions

Library of Congress Cataloging-in-Publication Data

Library of Congress Cataloging-in-Publication Data

Dolphin, Colleen, 1979-
  Volleyball by the numbers / Colleen Dolphin.
    p. cm. -- (Team sports by the numbers)
  ISBN 978-1-60453-772-7
  1. Volleyball--Juvenile literature. 2. Arithmetic--Juvenile literature. I. Title.
  GV1015.34.D65 2010
  796.325--dc22
                              2009029863

SandCastle™ Level: Fluent

SandCastle™ books are created by a team of professional educators, reading specialists, and content developers around five essential components—phonemic awareness, phonics, vocabulary, text comprehension, and fluency—to assist young readers as they develop reading skills and strategies and increase their general knowledge. All books are written, reviewed, and leveled for guided reading, early reading intervention, and Accelerated Reader® programs for use in shared, guided, and independent reading and writing activities to support a balanced approach to literacy instruction. The SandCastle™ series has four levels that correspond to early literacy development. The levels are provided to help teachers and parents select appropriate books for young readers.

| Emerging Readers | Beginning Readers | Transitional Readers | Fluent Readers |
| (no flags) | (1 flag) | (2 flags) | (3 flags) |

SandCastle™ would like to hear from you. Please send us your comments and suggestions.
sandcastle@abdopublishing.com

Contents

Introduction

Numbers are used all the time in volleyball.

- A volleyball net is 8 feet (2.4 m) high for men. It is 7 feet and 4 inches (2.2 m) high for women.

- A volleyball match has 2 **referees**. There are either 2 or 4 line judges.

- The lines on a volleyball court are 2 inches (5 cm) wide.

- The ceiling above a volleyball court must be at least 23 feet (7 m) high.

- An official volleyball weighs 9 to 10 ounces (255 to 283 g).

Let's learn more about how numbers are used in volleyball.

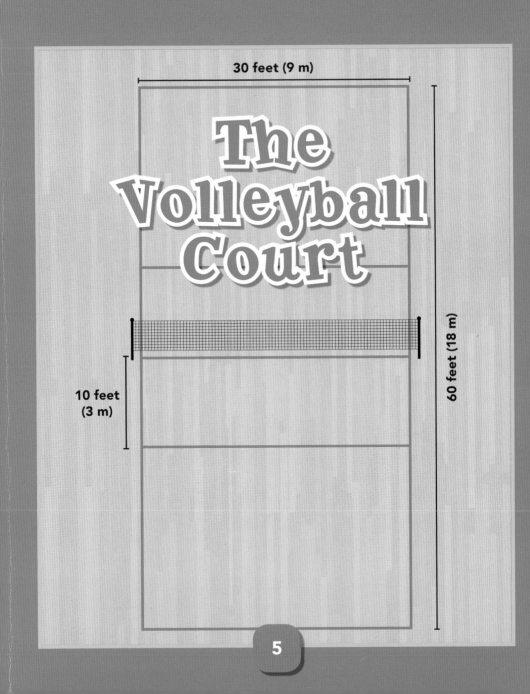

The Volleyball Court

30 feet (9 m)

60 feet (18 m)

10 feet (3 m)

The Game

A team can hit the ball up to 3 times. The third hit must **return** the ball over the net.

A volleyball match is made up of sets. A set is a game played to 25 points. The winning team must win by at least 2 points. The team that wins 3 sets wins the match.

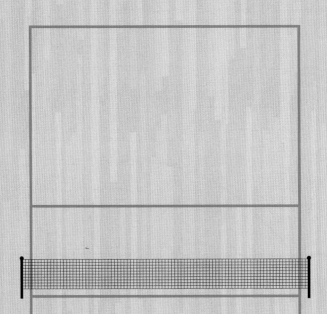

Right Front   **Center Front**   **Left Front**

Right Back   **Center Back**   **Left Back**

Offense

The team trying to score is the offense.

Anne gets ready to **serve** the ball.

By the Numbers!

(A) This is Anne's third serve in a row. If her team wins this point, Anne will serve the next point too. How many serves in a row will she have then?

(answer on p. 23)

Marissa passes the volleyball by **bumping** it to her teammate Sarah.

By the Numbers!

B Marissa hits the volleyball to Sarah. Then Sarah hits it over the net. How many times was the ball hit?

(answer on p. 23)

11

Kristine practices setting the volleyball.

C

Kristine is trying to set the ball 10 times in a row. She has already set the ball 7 times. How many more times does she need to set it?

(answer on p. 23)

Julian gets ready to **spike** the ball. He hopes to score a point for his team!

By the Numbers!

D Julian's team has 7 points. The other team has 5 points. How many more points does Julian's team have?

(answer on p. 23)

16

Defense

The team trying to keep the other team from scoring is the defense.

Sofia hit the ball over the net. William will try to **return** it.

By the Numbers!

E William hits the ball 1 time to return it over the net. The other team hits it 3 times. How many more times does the other team hit the ball?

(answer on p. 23)

Tony jumps up to block the ball! He keeps the other team from scoring.

F

Tony blocked the ball 5 times in the first set. He blocked the ball 3 times in the second set. How many total times did Tony block the ball?

(answer on p. 23)

Andy goes for a **dig**. He keeps the ball from hitting the ground.

By the Numbers!

G

Andy's team has won 2 sets. The other team has also won 2 sets. How many sets have they played?

(answer on p. 23)

Volleyball Facts

- William G. Morgan invented volleyball in 1895.

- Most players jump about 300 times during a volleyball match.

- A volleyball **marathon** lasted 75 hours and 30 minutes at Kingston, North Carolina.

- Over 800 million people around the world **participate** in volleyball.

- Volleyball was first included in the Olympic Games in 1964.

- In 1916, the set and **spike** offense was invented in the Philippines.

- The Volleyball Hall of Fame opened on June 6, 1987.

Answers to By the Numbers!

D

$$\begin{array}{r} 7 \\ -5 \\ \hline 2 \end{array}$$

Julian's team has 7 points. The other team has 5 points. How many more points does Julian's team have?

A

$$\begin{array}{r} 3 \\ +1 \\ \hline 4 \end{array}$$

This is Anne's third **serve** in a row. If her team wins this point, Anne will serve the next point too. How many serves in a row will she have then?

E

$$\begin{array}{r} 3 \\ -1 \\ \hline 2 \end{array}$$

William hits the ball 1 time to **return** it over the net. The other team hits it 3 times. How many more times does the other team hit the ball?

B

$$\begin{array}{r} 1 \\ +1 \\ \hline 2 \end{array}$$

Marissa hits the volleyball to Sarah. Then Sarah hits it over the net. How many times was the ball hit?

F

$$\begin{array}{r} 5 \\ +3 \\ \hline 8 \end{array}$$

Tony blocked the ball 5 times in the first set. He blocked the ball 3 times in the second set. How many total times did Tony block the ball?

C

$$\begin{array}{r} 10 \\ -7 \\ \hline 3 \end{array}$$

Kristine is trying to set the ball 10 times in a row. She has already set the ball 7 times. How many more times does she need to set it?

G

$$\begin{array}{r} 2 \\ +2 \\ \hline 4 \end{array}$$

Andy's team has won 2 sets. The other team has also won 2 sets. How many sets have they played?

Glossary

bump – to pass a volleyball by hitting it with your forearms.

dig – a volleyball play in which a player hits the ball just before it touches the ground.

marathon – a game, contest, or other activity that takes a very long time.

participate – to be a part of something.

referee – a person whose job is to make sure that the rules of a game are followed.

return – to hit the ball back over the net.

serve – to put the ball in play by hitting it over the net.

spike – in volleyball, to jump up and hit the ball hard to the other side of the net.

To see a complete list of SandCastle™ books and other nonfiction titles from ABDO Publishing Company, visit www.abdopublishing.com.
8000 West 78th Street, Edina, MN 55439 • 800-800-1312 • fax 952-831-1632